Off the Wall!

OFF THE WALL!

*School Year Bulletin Boards
and Displays for the Library*

by GAYLE SKAGGS

McFarland & Company, Inc., Publishers
Jefferson, North Carolina, and London

British Library Cataloguing-in-Publication data are available

Library of Congress Cataloguing-in-Publication Data

Skaggs, Gayle, 1952–
    Off the wall : school year bulletin boards and displays for the
library / by Gayle Skaggs.
      p. cm.
    ISBN 0-7864-0116-8 (sewn softcover : 55# alk. paper) ∞
    1. School libraries—United States. 2. Library exhibits—United
States. 3. Displays in education. 4. Bulletin boards—United
States. I. Title.
Z675.S3S5973 1995
027.8′0973—dc20   95-5693
                                                    CIP

Manufactured in the United States of America

McFarland & Company, Inc., Publishers
  Box 611, Jefferson, North Carolina 28640

This book is dedicated
to my best friend,
my husband, Bob

CONTENTS

INTRODUCTION

Do you dread changing your bulletin boards because you cannot think of anything new to make? Do you leave the same display up all year hoping no one will notice? This book is designed to provide you with new ideas for your display areas and stimulate your own creativity.

Display ideas such as hanging items from the ceiling on fishing line or placing displays in the center of the room will encourage you to stop thinking in a "flat" way and to start making your displays three-dimensional.

The ideas in this book are arranged to correlate with the school year, September through May. Over 100 bulletin boards and displays are presented with at least ten included for each month. Some of the ideas can be used at any time of the year while others are seasonal.

These ideas can be used as presented, or you can use your own creativity to adapt them to your library setting. Consider combining bits and pieces of several bulletin boards and displays to create an even better idea. Let your imagination go, and there will be no end to the exciting new environment created in your library.

CHAPTER 1

THE BASICS

Where do you start? Do you always do everything the same way? Well, stop! Begin by looking at the available space. If your bulletin board is small, why not go beyond the borders and use up an entire wall? If you usually decorate an entire wall, use only a portion of the area. The key is to vary what you do so that the displays are not predictable. The element of surprise is exciting.

Consider the area from all angles. Are you confined to a wall or can you use the ceiling, a support post, the windows? Try to really look at the room you have to work with in a new way.

It is not necessary to plan a display down to the very last detail. Some of the best displays just happen. Be flexible and enjoy the creating process.

When people walk into a room they are immediately struck by its color, or lack of it, and a library especially needs the excitement color can generate. Be bold and pump some life into your library with clean, bright colors.

Careful thought should be given to the cost of the materials needed for displays. Librarians seldom have enough money to spend on regular library materials, much less art supplies, so the key is to use whatever is available in the most creative way. One item that is really fantastic to use is carpet tubing. Tubing is thrown out by carpet stores, and store owners will gladly give you all you will take. A saw is required to cut the tubing, however.

The materials you use should be clean, bright, neat, and totally safe. Remember to recycle and reuse whenever possible. Store the display materials in plastic bags to keep the construction paper out of direct sunlight or other bright lighting. Construction paper fades easily. Use the pieces of displays over and over in new combinations.

Do not try to display a lot of things at one time. Keep the area uncluttered with a few well-placed displays that are changed frequently. Let your displays reflect your enthusiasm for reading and the library. Relax, enjoy yourself and soak up the compliments.

Backgrounds

Lots of materials work well for backgrounds. The following are just a few suggestions:

- Construction paper or poster paper.
- Newspaper — especially *The Wall Street Journal*.
- Old bed sheets — any color is great but light blue is the most practical.
- Black plastic bags — opened at the seams.
- Wallpaper — use leftovers or use pages from sample books.
- Brown mailing paper.
- Wrapping paper — gift wrap.
- Fabric — including burlap.
- Paper tablecloths — these are inexpensive and generally cover a large area.

Lettering

Poor lettering can kill an otherwise terrific display. Computers generate signs or letters if necessary, but one of the best ways to make letters is to use letter patterns and do it the old-fashioned way — cut them out! This does take time but the results are worth the effort. Letter patterns can be purchased inexpensively at school supply or office supply stores. Be sure to check your spelling.

The letter styles need to vary. Do not use the same type of letter for every display. (The lettering in this book was chosen for ease in making the drawings.) Substitute other letter styles for variety.

Visuals

Use an opaque projector if you have trouble drawing some of the items suggested. Use the idea of folding the paper and drawing half of the object on the fold. This is a terrific way to make a pattern for almost anything.

Hang items on fishing line. It is inexpensive and is almost invisible. Open up a paper clip to use as a hook to attach your artwork to a light fixture or ceiling tile.

Try to use your school mascot whenever possible. Many ideas that are included in this book feature a jaybird named Jasper. He is the mascot of Jefferson City High School, Jefferson City, Missouri, where the school colors are red and black. Substitute your mascot and your school colors. Personalize the displays because your patrons will notice.

CHAPTER 2

SEPTEMBER

WELCOME BACK

(opposite)

Use a black background to simulate a chalkboard. Giant white letters greet your patrons.

Beside a giant red construction paper apple, add a king-sized tape measure. This is easy to make. Use $12'' \times 18''$ sheets of yellow construction paper carefully taped together. Use a ruler to mark off the tape with one foot equaling one inch. Draw the lines in with a  black marker. Use silver paper or aluminum foil to create an end for the tape measure. This tape measure can be as long as you desire. Pin it on the bulletin board and drape it loosely up and over and around the display area.

The pencils can be of any color. Even though they are flat pieces of construction paper, a few carefully placed folds will give them a 3-D look. The body of the pencil is a long rectangle of any color construction paper.

A pink triangle is glued on the end of the rectangle. Color the lead in with a black marker. Add a pink rectangle with one end rounded off for the pencil's eraser. Wrap silver paper or aluminum foil to cover where the pencil and eraser meet. Use a black marker for details.

Fold the long rectangle twice completely from one end to the other.

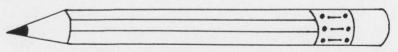

When you pin this onto the bulletin board, pin only the edges so that the pencil will curve out and look more realistic.

You might personalize these pencils with your school's name or the name of your school's mascot. The pencils and the tape measure are also useable for the display idea "Time to Make Big Plans to Use Your Library More This Year" (see page 10).

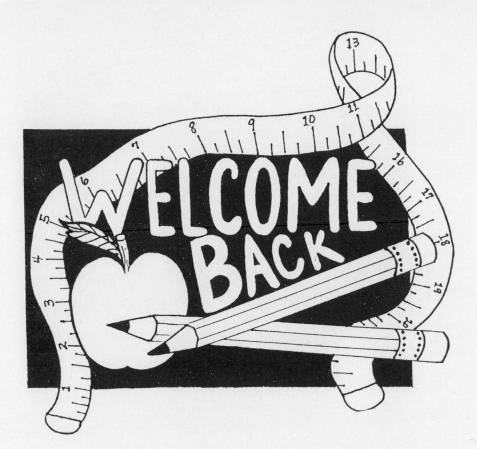

TIME TO MAKE BIG PLANS

(shown on page 10)

This is a very graphic design that gets the message across in a "big" way. It is a good way to begin the year. Use a light color for the background of this large display. (This will require quite a bit of space.) Use the pencils and tape measure described in the "Welcome Back" display. Substitute your school mascot for the Jaybird. Feature the mascot with a book covered in a school book cover and be sure to include a wristwatch to emphasize the word "time."

Two sizes of letters are needed. Use larger letters for the main message and slightly smaller letters for each of the three other statements.

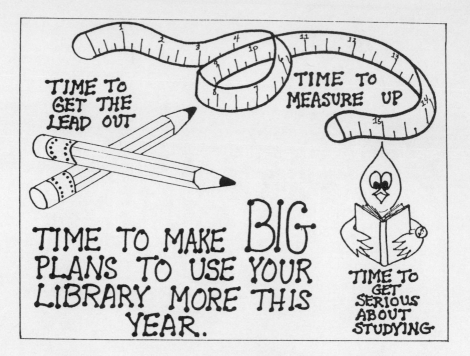

PENCILS

(opposite)

These large pencils are lots of fun and are great attention-getters. If you are constantly having to point out the pencil sharpener, hang one of these large pencils to point the way.

The pencils are made from a piece of carpet tube. These tubes are easy to get from any carpet store and are free.

Cut the tube the length you would like your pencil to be. You will probably need a saw to do this.

To make the point section of the pencil, roll a piece of 12″ × 18″ pink construction paper into a cone and staple it together. Use a black marker to color in the point. Put some small wads of newspaper into the cone to fill it up and this will help to keep its shape. Tape the cone over the end of the tube. Be sure it fits tightly.

The eraser is made by pulling a sheet of pink paper over the end of the tube and taping it in place. Carefully fold it down as smoothly as possible.
Wrap another long rectangle of pink paper
around this even with the end of the tube. This
will cover up the pleats you will have had to
make. Staple or tape in place.

Use any color paper for the middle section of the pencil. Your school colors always work well. Depending upon the size of your pencil, this will probably be a rather large sheet of paper.

Use silver paper or aluminum foil trimmed up with a black marker for the ferrule of the pencil.

Letters cut from construction paper and glued on will add the finishing touch. If you use a marker to write the words, you must be very careful. It is so much easier to glue words on than to replace the whole sheet of paper.

WELCOME WREATH

(opposite)

Fall is a great time to go with an apple theme and use lots of bright red to boldly begin the new school year.

Make a pattern for the apple shape so the apples will be uniform in appearance. The apples can be flat or stapled together to add a more 3-D effect. Just staple through the center and fold the two halves to the center. Do not be afraid to even add a worm.

Fill in the space between the apples with green leaves. Finish up the wreath with a large bow and a big "Welcome" for the center.

To expand the apple theme in the library, hang a branch from the ceiling using fishing line. Then hang apple shapes from the limbs and tack on some green leaves. You can incorporate the display on the following page to go all out for a total apple blitz of your library.

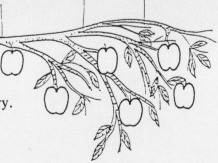

APPLE TREE

(opposite)

This fall display can be large enough to set on the floor or scaled down for a table top. Use a tree branch firmly planted in a pot or tub. It is very important that the branch is really secure in the pot because of safety, and you do not want all your decorating efforts to end up on the floor.

The apples for the tree can be red construction paper apple shapes, or you can photocopy the covers of some of your new books on red copy paper and cut them into apple shapes. These can be hung with fishing line. Add some red bows (red plaid is nice) to fill up the tree.

Display books ready for checkout at the bottom of the tree. Bushel baskets turned upside down will allow you some great display space and seem quite appropriate.

A simple message—READ—can be added to the container holding the tree. If you do not want to use apples, substitute leaves.

The apple theme can be expanded to include some apple swags hung throughout the library. Cut some apple shapes and tie them together with ribbon or macrame cord. Use a paper punch to make neat holes. Cut out letters and glue them on the apples to create your message.

All the apples do not have to be exactly the same. Take a bite out of one every once in a while for variety.

WELCOME

(shown on page 16)

This is a very graphic design that will boldly welcome people to your library.

Use a black background to simulate a blackboard. Use white letters with the word "Welcome" in the largest letters.

Add a couple of simple apples

made from red construction paper with brown stems and green leaves. You might consider hanging additional apples from the ceiling area directly in front of the bulletin board.

START THE YEAR FRESH

(opposite)

Make a tree from brown mailing paper or from cardboard. Use a brown and a black marker to simulate bark. A few simple lines can really give the bark some texture.

Use green tissue paper or construction paper for leaves. The leaves could be cut individually and pinned on or cut as a whole section at one time. This would almost look like a green cloud.

The apple shapes can be made from red construction paper, or you can photocopy the covers of some of your new books on red copy paper and cut them into apple shapes. If you opt for the construction paper, use a marker to write the title and call number of one of your new books on each apple. Hang these shapes from the ceiling directly in front of the bulletin board using fishing line or pin into place on the tree. If you hang some apples from the ceiling, it will seem that you are actually walking under the tree.

START THE YEAR FRESH. PICK ONE OF OUR NEW BOOKS.

READING ADDS COLOR TO YOUR LIFE

(opposite)

Color is really an attention-getter so start the year off boldly. Think big as you plan to use this idea. It has a black background to capitalize on the color contrast. The word "Welcome" works well if done in big red letters.

The paint brush is made from brown mailing paper. Roll the paper lengthwise and tape shut.

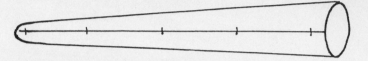

One end of the tube should be larger than the other end. Close off the small end to create the end of the brush handle. Use more brown wrapping paper to make the bristles. Fold the paper in half and draw the bristle lines in with a black marker. Staple the two sheets 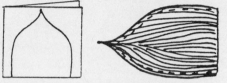 together and put a small amount of newspaper inside for padding. Fold the bristles and tape to the open end of the brush handle.

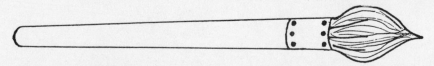

Use a piece of silver paper or aluminum foil to wrap around the brush to cover up the point where the bristles meet the handle. Use a black marker to add some details. Red construction paper can be added to the bristles to simulate red paint. Be sure to add a few drips for a little extra color.

The center of the board is the artist's palette. Brown wrapping paper works well for this. Assign a color for each type of book and cut the letters from that color. The word "Library" should be in red. This is just symbolic and is for the word "Read." Use the correct color paper to match the book category and photocopy the covers of some of your new books. For example, blue for biographies, orange for mystery, and so on. Scatter these covers throughout the display.

The remaining letters work well in white except for the word "Color." Choose five of the colors you have already used and cut one letter from each until you have spelled out "Color" in some real color.

NEW BOOKS

(opposite)

If you would like a simple way to draw attention to new materials in your library, try one of these. These ideas work well with the bulletin board "Reading Adds Color to Your Life." Use paint cans, brushes, drop cloths, an easel, and a ladder to support the theme.

Use the easel to announce your new books. Put a drop cloth down on the table before you begin to display the books. Empty paint cans (or full if you want to use new cans) might serve as bookends. You can even make new labels for these cans like "Library Read" or put labels on the cans to match your color designation for the "Reading Adds Color to Your Life" bulletin board. Place some paint brushes around for an extra touch.

If space is available, set up a stepladder and place new books on the steps and on the floor. A paint can sitting at the base of the ladder can serve to hold up a book for display.

COLORFUL CRAYONS

(shown on page 22)

This idea can be utilized with the other "color" display described in the September chapter or used alone. Everyone loves crayons.

Make the box out of yellow paper, and try to make it match a real crayon box as much as possible. This is a pop art display that all your patrons will be able to relate to.

The box will be flat while the crayons in the front can be pinned on in such a way as to appear 3-D.

Each crayon represents a type of book in the library. You designate the colors for each area. Each crayon is a rectangle and a triangle of the same color. Start with the rectangle. Round off one end. Use a marker for drawing in details.

Cut a triangle with the base the same size as the end of the rectangle. Add a small rectangle to the base of the triangle.

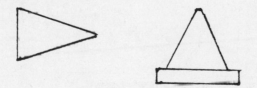

Glue these pieces together. Cut a rectangle from a contrasting color paper to use as a label. Cut letters from dark construction paper and glue on to signify a kind of book (for example, Mystery). Pin these crayons on so that they appear to be rounded with the pins along the very outside edges only.

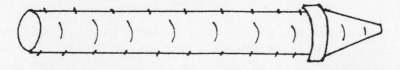

READ...PUT MORE COLOR IN YOUR LIFE

(opposite)

Use a black background with large letters of red paper. Create a crayon for the bulletin board as described in the previous plan. To make the hanging crayon, use a carpet tube. Cut the tube the length you would like your crayon to be. You will need a saw to do this. Choose a color for the crayon. Start with the ends of the crayon. Use a sheet of 12″ × 18″ paper for the point end. Roll this paper into a cone and staple it shut. Put small wads of newspaper into the cone to fill it up (this will help to keep its shape). Tape it in place.

Fold another 12″ × 18″ sheet of the same color paper over the other end of the tube. Carefully fold it down and tape it into place. Use another rectangle of the same color to wrap around the tube to cover up the folds and give a smooth appearance to the crayon. Be sure this piece is even with the end of the tube.

Use a larger sheet of a contrasting color paper to wrap around the tube for the crayon's label. Be sure this covers all the tape on both ends. Cut letters and glue them on for the word "Fiction."

Photocopy book covers of fiction books on paper to match the color you chose for the fiction crayon. Do the same for nonfiction. Make some additional crayons to use around the room for added color. Have fun with them.

GET IN STEP THIS YEAR

(opposite)

Creating these legs is fairly easy. Use a solid color background and concentrate the detail work on the legs and shoes.

The first legs are just rectangles. To make the shoes, take a man's shoe and lay it on its side and trace around it. Draw in the details. Use an indefinite shape to fill in the space between the pants and the shoes. Add some vertical lines to turn this space into a pair of socks.

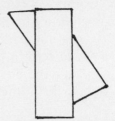

If you do not want to tackle the other legs, just make them all like the first pair and substitute in tennis shoes and blue jeans. Fold the paper and cut out two at the same time.

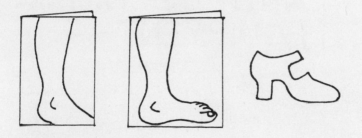

Do not get hung up on realism. Funny legs are great.

Carry the shoe theme throughout the library by using old shoes as pencil holders, or put a plant in an old tennis shoe. The rubber sole will hold water, and this planter will become quite a conversation piece.

START THE YEAR WITH
THE PROPER EQUIPMENT

(below)

This is a quick display idea. All you need is an old book bag, some library books, and some construction paper letters.

Any color background is good, but this would be a great opportunity to zero in on your school's colors.

Tack the book bag to the bulletin board firmly and put some paperbacks in the pockets. Keep it simple.

NATIONAL DOG WEEK

(shown on page 28)

Use a table or bookcase top to display books about dogs including fiction and nonfiction during the last week of September.

Create a simple doghouse if you have enough display space. Make the doghouse out of a box which you will paint or cover with paper. A triangle will need to be added on each end. To make this shape the correct size, cut a rectangle of cardboard the same length as the end of the box. Measure across halfway and make a mark at the top. Use a ruler to draw a line from this mark to each of the two bottom corners. Cut out the triangle, and use it as a pattern to make another one for the other end of the box. Use duct tape to position the pieces into place.

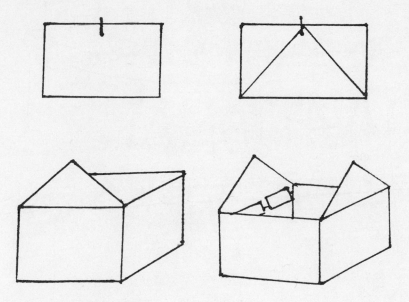

Use a large cardboard rectangle folded in half for the gable roof. Either paint a hole for a doorway or cut one out. Use a stuffed dog and some footprints.

Hang a sign with some "doggie" message. Foam insulation board is easy to cut and weighs almost nothing. Use fishing line to hang your sign.

CHAPTER 3

OCTOBER

JOPLIN, Mo. (AP) — Marlene Agan often travels alone — with no qualms.

"I've [found] ... [waiting] ... someone ... I might wait for ... There ... [I] went to see and do ... now," the Joplin ... said.

According to the U.S. Travel Data Center, Ms. Agan is one of ... [million] travelers who ... 1992, have ... [at least 10] ... been the same ... and home ... [leisure] trips.

But while single travelers make up a sizable por- tion of the vacation mark..., they still feel like extra baggage when it comes to paying the cost of a solo vacation.

"They're convinced [they're] being penalized or traveling alone," said Robert Whitely, president of the U.S. Tour Operators Association.

The No. 1 gripe among singles by far is the prac- tice of charging supplementary fees for one person using a double-occupancy room. Single travelers often ... percent more than some- one sharing a ...

"The travel industry is primarily [geared] for cou- ples," said Ed Perks of Consumer Reports Travel Letter. "What ... is ...

Nancy Rob[erts] ... of Carthage compared rates for a 7-night vacation on

ed the same package, he or she would pay $2,023 ...

"Normally, a single pays 150 percent of the do ... occupancy rate," she said.

To ... each ... many sales ... or r ... while Ms. oth ... [groups] ... [intermodal] ... she said.

Gavin, " ... [outside]," of Single ... [International] ... [company] ... [isn't] a dating se ... but rather ... compatible t ... [dates].

One of the largest travel-matching services il ... [works] ... or asks its clients to fill out ap ... [great] questions about their age, occup ...

"We find out if they are day people or night pe ... Do they smoke or not? What type of entertain ... do they like?" van der Merwe said.

About 9,000 singles a year use Singleworld, w ... also offers travel packages for singles, such as ranch vacations and African safaris.

... the matching se ... trip ... Noth[ing] ... it alone.

... travel pack ... [places] like Mexico and the Caribbean, whic ... [include] all me ... accommodations, e ... [entertainment] ... [Ironically] ... [there's] more new p ... when he travels alone than when he's with frien[ds].

WHAT'S BLACK AND WHITE AND READ ("red") ALL OVER? THIS IS NATIONAL NEWSPAPER WEEK!

NATIONAL NEWSPAPER WEEK

(opposite)

This event is celebrated during the first week of October. Use a *Wall Street Journal* and some construction paper letters to spell out this old riddle.

Put a colorful sign by your newspapers to call attention to them. Encourage your teachers to use the papers for a classroom assignment, or ask a daily trivia question from the newspaper with a prize for the first student with the correct answer.

WELCOME TO YOUR LIBRARY

(shown on page 32)

This display is simple but can add just the right touch for fall. Cut leaves from construction paper or use real leaves that you have pressed. Pin them on the bulletin board being sure to bend and twist them to create a 3-D effect. Add a colorful bow (plaid is nice).

If you think the wreath looks too skimpy, just add another row of leaves. The letters can circle the wreath instead of being on the bottom. Try it both ways and see which you like best. You will be impressed with your handiwork.

READ

(shown on page 32)

Fall is such a beautiful time of the year. Use a bright blue background for some colorful leaves made from red, yellow, orange and brown construction paper.

If leaves are difficult for you to make, trace around some real leaves. Use several different types such as maple and oak, and use a marker to add the veins.

Arrange the leaves to spell out "Read," and include some book covers or magazine covers to encourage your patrons to read just for the fun of it.

LEAVES

(below)

Use large sheets of red, yellow, orange and brown construction paper to create giant-sized leaves to hang from the ceiling and on the windows.

If you have trouble making a large leaf, enlarge a real leaf on the copy machine to create a pattern. Use a variety of leaves.

A fancier leaf can be made by cutting out sections of the leaf and covering the space in amber-colored cellophane. Hanging these from the ceiling will require you to make them look nice from both sides. Glue the two sheets of construction paper leaves together with the cellophane in the middle.

Create a lovely banner by using a large sheet of construction paper folded at the top to form a casing. Hang this with fishing line. Add a message and decorate with leaves. These banners could be made to call attention to each Dewey area throughout the library.

Use the leaves liberally. Let color fall all over the room.

COLUMBUS

(below)

Use this bulletin board to encourage your students to think about Columbus and to read more about him. Display books reflecting both opinions of him, and be ready to discuss briefly why he might be considered a villain. This might be a new idea to some.

Any color background is suitable. Use a world map cut into a circle to represent the earth. Feature the Atlantic Ocean area.

Make a small ship from brown construction paper with a few white sails. Keep the boat very simple. Position the boat right in the middle of the Atlantic heading toward the New World. Finish up the display with bold letters, preferably in black.

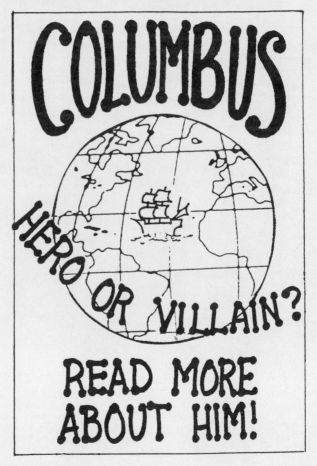

PUMPKIN WREATH

(shown on page 36)

Create this wreath using orange construction paper and paper cut into fall leaves or real leaves you have pressed. Use a black marker to draw in the faces and add brown paper stems. All of the jack-o'-lanterns do not need to have the same expression. Be creative.

Green paper ribbon comes twisted tightly and can be purchased very inexpensively at craft stores. Wrap it around a pencil to create the curly twists to add to the pumpkins. Thin strips of green construction paper wrapped around a pencil can achieve the same effect.

Four pumpkins is not the magic number. Make as many as you wish and create a larger wreath. Fill in with the leaves. If you use construction paper leaves, use red, brown, orange and yellow. Draw in details with the black marker. If you have trouble making leaves, trace around some real maple or oak leaves.

Add a large bow. Relax and wait for the compliments.

Carry on your pumpkin theme with some pumpkin swags. Tie paper pumpkins together with paper ribbon or twine. These will brighten up any size space.

These bats are a snap to make. Fold a sheet of $12'' \times 18''$ black paper in half. Draw half of the bat on the fold. Cut it out while still folded. Open out and hang on fishing line from the ceiling or the venetian blinds. Any little breeze will cause them to sail around. Tape a piece of wire or a straw to the back and stick the bat in a plant.

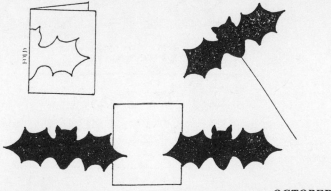

IT'S A MYSTERY...

(opposite)

This is a great display that will take almost no time to prepare. Begin with a black background. The words can be done in white or orange letters.

Photocopy the covers of some mystery books or use book covers. Use purchased spider webs throughout to tie everything together. These spider webs tend to move around as people walk past the display, and the movement adds a lot of character.

A spider or two will add a lot to the Halloween atmosphere. This one is made with a gum ball (seed pod) as the center. Add black pipe cleaner legs glued in place and a black pompon for the head. Add a pair of eyes, and glue a piece of elastic thread to the top of the gum ball so that the spider will bounce. Position it in the web, and then just wait for the comments.

IT'S A MYSTERY
WHY MORE PEOPLE DON'T READ!

SPOOKY TALES

(below)

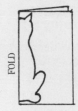

Begin with a black background complete with a bright orange or yellow full moon and some large construction paper books for the cat to sit on. The open book can be blank, or you might enlarge a couple of pages from a scary story book.

Begin the cat silhouette by making a pattern using a sheet of newspaper folded in half. Decide how large you would like the cat to be and draw half of the shape on the fold. Cut out the shape while the paper is still folded. Open it out and trace the cat pattern on black construction paper.

Cut a tail and glue it into place. Glue on some whiskers, too.

'TIS THE SEASON FOR SPOOKY TALES

(shown on page 40)

Use a black background and white letters. The letters for "Spooky Tales" should be cut to look spooky. Use regular letter patterns and alter the edges to look wavy.

The ghosts are made from cheesecloth which can be purchased at any fabric store for very little. One yard is enough to make a ghost. Sew a casing in one end. This material will ravel easily so fold the end over and stitch carefully in place.

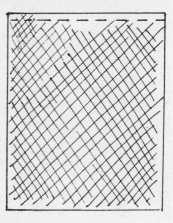

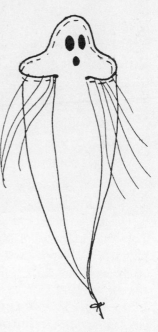

Straighten out a clothes hanger and bend it into this shape. Be sure to bend the ends of the wire into a loop so that there will be no sharp points. Use white spray paint to paint the hanger.

Slide the fabric over the wire form. Use white thread to tack the ends of the cheesecloth to the ends of the wire. Add extra strips of cheesecloth for the hands to blow around and be spooky.

Glue on two large black circles of felt or construction paper for eyes and a smaller black circle for the mouth. Fasten in a lightweight book or magazine. Hang the ghost with fishing line.

READ IN PEACE

(opposite)

Use a black background to showcase a purchased skeleton. It is possible to make the skeleton, but I recommend that you buy one. They are inexpensive and such a time saver. Use a gray construction paper rectangle with one end rounded off to create a tombstone for your reclining skeleton to lean against. Use a strip of brown paper for the ground.

Spread around some spider webs and add a book. This is so easy. You will be able to Relax In Peace with a good bulletin board.

SCARECROW

(shown on page 42)

Use a brown bag, some newspaper, some old clothes, and a lawn chair to make this display. If space is a problem, skip the chair and position the figure on top of a bookcase out of the way.

Make the head by stuffing a brown grocery bag half full with newspaper. Tie a yardstick and a ruler together as in the picture below. Slide the bag over the top of the yardstick and tie into place. Use a marker to draw in the face.

Put the shirt on your newly created ruler shoulders. Button up the front and stuff with newspapers. Stuff a pair of gloves and pin them to the bottom of the sleeves. Stuff the pants, and stuff the cuffs into a pair of boots. These may have to be taped together.

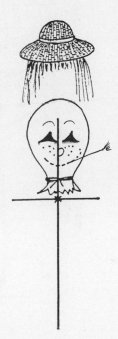

(SCARECROW, continued)

Tie a scarf around the neck and position the figure comfortably in the lawn chair. It may be necessary to tie the figure to the chair to keep it sitting up. Add a hat with a wig attached or use paper twist ribbon taped to the top of the brown bag.

Give your scarecrow something to read, and place more books around the chair. Add a construction paper crow if desired.

CHAPTER 4

NOVEMBER

WHO'S YOUR FAVORITE AUTHOR?

(below)

Create a gigantic book complete with a book-reading book-worm. Be colorful and silly.

Ask faculty and staff members to tell you their favorite author or favorite book. Computer generate these and display them all around the library. Feature many of these favorite books, and encourage your students to read them and then to go and talk to the faculty members about them. It is great for the students to find that they share a favorite book with possibly their favorite teacher. This is also a good opportunity for you to take a little inventory to see if your library has a copy of the favorite books.

YOUR STATE'S AUTHORS

(opposite)

This display is designed to call attention to the authors of your state and encourage your students to read their books. Possibly, you could coordinate this display with a visit by a local author to generate more interest.

Cut out a large outline of your state. Any color scheme is great. The actual names work well if they are done on a computer for uniformity. (Obviously, there are too many letters to cut them out of construction paper.) Position the author's name next to the area of the state the author is from.

Pull books by these authors and create a display to make it easier for the students to find the books. Add some nonfiction books to the display, too.

DEMOCRAT VS. REPUBLICAN

(below)

Use November, especially in election years, to showcase books on politics, government, past elections, and political campaigns. You can also showcase political cartoons and humor.

Set up a book display using lots of red, white and blue 4th of July decorations. Write to each party headquarters for information on party platform. Do not push one party over the other—just equally present information on Republicans and Democrats.

VOTE

(below)

Use a carpet tube or two duct-taped oatmeal boxes for the body of this Uncle Sam. He looks great sitting with books about politics and government.

Start with the face area. Wrap a rectangle of pink construction paper around the tube. Draw the eyes, a nose, a moustache, and hair. To make the hat, fold a sheet of blue paper over the end of the tube. Tape in place. Use a rectangle of striped paper to cover the area of tape making sure the top of the paper is even with the edge of the tube. This striped paper can be wrapping paper or white paper. Draw vertical lines with a red and a blue marker.

To make the brim of the hat, trace the end of the tube onto a sheet of blue paper. Use a compass to make the circle at least two inches wider and form a ring. Slide the ring over the tube, and tape it carefully on the underneath side.

Wrap striped paper around the bottom of the tube for the pants. Use blue for the vest and add lick-and-stick stars. Cut two long, thin blue rectangles for arms (plus some pink hands). Cut a piece of black paper for the shoes. This shape is almost a heart shape with the point rounded off. Tape it to the bottom of the tube.

Add a bow tie. Give Uncle Sam a sign to hold encouraging everyone to vote.

WHERE IN THE WORLD HAVE YOU BEEN?

(below)

National Geography Week needs to be promoted, and this display is a whiz to put up.

Use a world map and encourage your patrons to put a marker in the countries they have visited. Provide colored stick pens that will show up on the map.

Display travel books from all parts of the world and consider asking a geography question each day with a small prize for the winner. Show travel videos before and after school or put up some posters from local travel consultants.

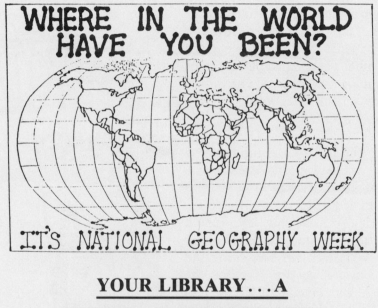

YOUR LIBRARY...A

BOUNTY OF INFORMATION

(opposite)

This display can be made to accommodate any size space. Create the cornucopia first. Use a piece of cardboard cut into a cornucopia shape. Cut strips of brown paper and loosely cover the cardboard attaching the strips only at the top and bottom on the back of the cardboard. You are actually creating a paper loom.

Use long strips of brown paper to weave through the shorter strips and attach them to the back of the cardboard. You should end up with a woven basket look. Use a circle of brown paper to slide into the open end to make it look 3-D and round. When you pin this on the bulletin board, bend the cardboard slightly to give it a curved appearance. Use pins only on the outside edges.

Use all types of media along with paper fruit and leaves to fill the cornucopia. A big paper ribbon bow helps to fill up the space also.

Your Library...
a bounty of information.

THANKSGIVING PUMPKINS

(shown on page 50)

Do you have a couple of good looking pumpkins left over from Halloween? Even if you have painted a face on one side, consider using the back of the pumpkin to create an Indian or a pilgrim.

For the Indian, paint the back and sides of the pumpkin black for hair. Paint on two circles for eyes, a sideways horseshoe for the nose and a big smile. Use red paint or a red marker for some war paint.

Use a strip of construction paper to make the headband. Use markers to add some colorful designs.

Use a real feather or a construction paper feather.

The pilgrim needs hair painted on just as the Indian. Paint on a similar face.

Set the pumpkin on a sheet of white paper cut to resemble a collar. Purchase a pilgrim style hat at a party shop or hobby shop. A hat can be made from construction paper but it is not easy.

READ PERIODICALLY

(shown on page 52)

This turkey will brighten up any area with his tail made of magazine covers. Ask your friends to save for you the covers from some of their magazines, and try to come up with an equal number that are appealing to females and to males.

The turkey head, wings and legs are made from construction paper. The head/body is shaped like a bowling pin and is made from brown paper. Add a beak, eyes and wattle. Use a black marker to draw in the feathers and other details.

The wings can be made by folding a sheet of brown paper. Draw one wing and then cut it out while the paper is still folded. This will give you two wings that are the same. Attach the wings to the body.

The legs are the funniest part. Use two long sheets of brown paper. Draw one leg, cut it out, turn it upside down, and trace around it for the second leg. Use a marker to jazz it up. Tape the legs to the back of the body.

Give your turkey a magazine to read. Have fun selecting a title. Add an appropriate message.

ANOTHER TURKEY!

(shown on page 52)

Using a straw wreath, create this turkey for a bulletin board or door. The size of the turkey will depend on the size of the straw wreath.

Fill the wreath from top to bottom with bright construction paper feathers. Fasten them on the back so that the hole is completely covered.

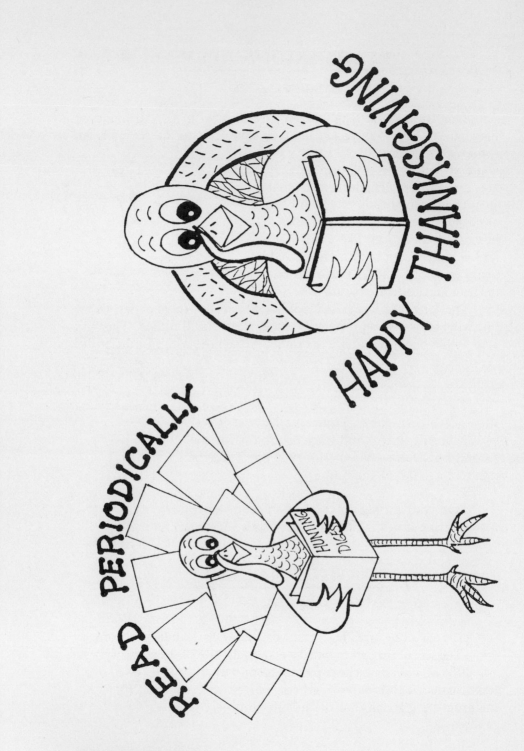

Follow the instructions given for "Read Periodically" to make the head, wings, eyes, etc.

Use duct-tape or straight pins to attach the body to the wreath. It will not weigh much. Add a book (possibly a cookbook). Add an appropriate message.

To hang this on the door, use a loop of wire at the top of the back of the wreath.

PAPER BAG TURKEY

(shown on page 54)

Do you want a really cheap Thanksgiving decorating idea? All you need is a large, brown grocery bag. Fill the bag about half-full with wadded-up newspaper. Close up the bag with a rubberband. Fluff out the end of the bag to create the tail section.

Use construction paper to make the rest of the turkey. The head is shaped like a cotton swab on one end and fanned out on the other. Add two eyes and a beak. Use a strip of red paper with the corners rounded off to glue by the beak.

Glue all the turkey face parts together, and glue the head onto the brown bag. Cut two wings from dark brown construction paper and glue into place.

Use some earthy colors for the tail feathers. Glue these onto the fanned-out section of the brown bag. Use a brown or black marker to add some details. A few lines drawn somewhat like brick work will give the impression of feathers on the front of your turkey.

HAPPINESS IS HOMEMADE

(below)

Set up a display of craft books to encourage your patrons to try something new. Place a quilt on the table and add simple tools, yarn, and paintbrushes. Use foam insulation board for a sign to call attention to your display.

If you have a display case that can be locked, include some handmade items along with books describing how to make them.

This is a good display to use before the holidays to encourage your patrons to make gifts for the holidays. This is an opportunity to make a statement against all the commercialism of Christmas and at the same time encourage others to give a part of themselves.

CHAPTER 5

DECEMBER

RUDOLPH WREATH

(opposite)

This display is easy and inexpensive to make, and it will add some humor to your holiday decorating. Rudolph could really hang anywhere, but if he adorns a bulletin board, use a bold background of Christmas red or a bold blue with a few small snowflakes or stars scattered around to depict a sky perfect for a sleigh ride.

Use a brown paper bag turned inside out or some brown construction paper for the head, ears and feet. The antlers can be the same color as the head or a darker brown if you desire.

The head is just a large light bulb shape. The ears are triangles with the bottom rounded off.

Fold the paper for the antlers lengthwise so that you can cut both at the same time. Glue these on the back of the head. The antlers will probably need a little reinforcement to keep them up. Try taping a straw on the back side. Just for fun wrap some red ribbon with little jingle bells around the antlers.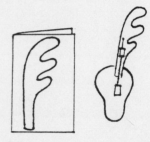

Cut two large white circles and two small black circles for eyes. The nose could be a large shiny red Christmas ball, a red yarn ball or fringe ball, a red shiny bow, a red foil circle, or a foam ball painted red or covered in red ribbon. There are endless possibilities for this nose.

The feet are simple shapes folded around a book, a Christmas card, or even a sign with a Christmas greeting from your staff.

The wreath itself works well if artificial greenery is wound into a circle, or cardboard holly leaves could be used and bunched together to form the wreath. Try something different each year using the same reindeer and see how different the effect is.

Do not worry about realism — just go for fun and get a giggle out of your patrons.

Flight Manu

MERRY CHRISTMAS

MERRY CHRISTMAS

(shown on page 60)

These toy soldiers, who are busily guarding your Christmas books, can be made from several oatmeal boxes or coffee cans duct-taped together or from pieces of carpet tubing. Decorate the soldier with construction paper, aluminum foil, ribbon, or wrapping paper, and do the detail work with a marker.

Begin with the face area and then add the hair followed by the hat. To make the crown of the hat, carefully tape a square of paper over the end of the tube. Use a rectangle of paper to wrap around the tube covering the tape.

It is important to begin and end on the back each time you add a new strip of paper. Be as neat as possible. You will want the back to look nice because your soldier may be sitting in an area where he will be viewed from all sides.

Add a strip of construction paper for the pants and the shirt. The shoes are just half circles, and the line separating the legs is done in marker.

Be sure to add a flap on the arms so you will be able to attach them to the body.

The large-sized candy can be made from half-inch white foam insulation board. This is so easy to cut with a matt knife. Wrap the candy cane in wide red ribbon. The piece of striped candy is made from a piece of foam painted in stripes or a solid color. Wrap the candy in cellophane. If you use colored cellophane, you really do not have to paint the foam. The cellophane or plastic wrapped around the candy gives it a "real" look.

Hang the finished candy on fishing line. Add an appropriate holiday message.

VICTORIAN CHRISTMAS

(shown on page 62)

These two Santas look wonderful hanging around the library. Be sure to make them look good from both sides.

Both Santas are made from construction paper. Use a deep red color rather than a bright Christmas red. For the fur use polyester fiberfil or white construction paper. Add some white glitter to sparkle as they move around in the breeze. If the designs are a little too difficult, enlarge them on the copy machine to make some patterns. Keep them simple.

The street light is made from a carpet tube which sits on a base made from wood scraps. The two arms are cut from cardboard. Be sure to add a flap that can be inserted in a slit made in the tube.

Paint the tube, stand and cardboard arms black. Use white balloons for the street light bulbs. Use fishing line to tie the balloons to the end of the cardboard arm. Decorate with evergreen and ribbon.

MERRY READING CHRISTMAS TREE

(shown on page 64)

This festive tree can be made any size with the tree serving as the focal point. Use a bright red or blue background.

Begin the tree with two large sheets of green paper the size you want your tree to be. Fold a sheet of paper lengthwise. Draw half of the tree on the fold. Cut the tree out while the paper is still folded. Open it out and trace around it on the second sheet of paper. Cut it out.

Staple the two sheets of paper together down the center. You can staple the tree directly onto the bulletin board. Fold the two top pieces so that they stand out from the board. Now your tree has some shape. Use a brown rectangle for the tree trunk.

String popcorn, foam pieces, or regular Christmas tinsel around your tree. Use paper decorations or real ornaments to finish up the tree. Use photocopies of book covers or book jackets as gifts.

MERRY READING

(shown on page 64)

If you do not have a great display area and need all your table space, get a washer or dryer box from an appliance store to use for a free-standing holiday display space. To reinforce the top of the box, you might want to use strong tape around the edges, or you can cut another piece of heavy cardboard the same size and set it on top to create a harder, steadier surface.

Wrap the box in some Christmas paper and, of course, add ribbon and a large bow. You could add a gift tag with season's greetings

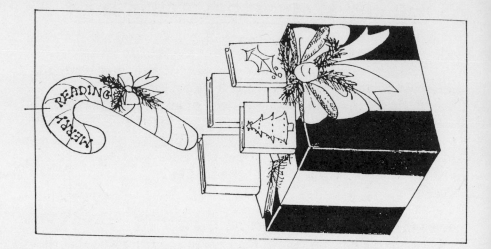

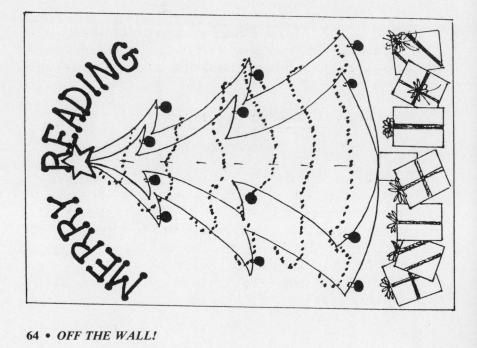

from your staff and possibly even some greenery or ornaments. You now have your display area for those beautiful holiday books.

Use foam insulation board to make a sign. This could be any one of the traditional holiday shapes like a candy cane, star, bell, or holly leaf. Use the same ribbon on the shape as you did on the gift box for continuity.

<u>HAPPY HOLIDAYS</u>

(shown on page 66)

This idea incorporates a star theme throughout the library. The wreath is simply evergreen with stars added. Use foil wrapping paper. Consider using plaid foil, if possible. The plaid gives the stars an unusual look that is very appealing.

Make a pattern for the star from newspaper so that all the stars will be the same size. If you have trouble making a star, trace around a star cookie cutter and enlarge it on the copy machine.

Once you have cut the stars out of the foil, fold them. Find the center and fold out to each point. Also fold from the center to the spot where each arm of the star comes together. This will help the stars to stand out from the wreath and have more body and shape.

(HAPPY HOLIDAYS, continued)

A bow is optional but do add an appropriate message.

Set up a display table of Christmas books. Hang stars of different colors, including the plaid foil ones, from the ceiling and tape them on the table covering. Large, empty boxes wrapped in Christmas paper serve well to help display books if you are needing more space.

Cut star shapes from construction paper and cut out the center of each star. Fill in this space with colored cellophane or aluminum foil. Hang these from the ceiling or put them on the windows.

This is a really inexpensive way to decorate, but the foil paper gives it pizazz.

CHRISTMAS ORNAMENT

(opposite)

This display can be one large ornament on the bulletin board or done as many ornaments hung from the ceiling. Use foil paper for the background with aluminum foil or silver paper for the top closer. The foil paper gives the display the shiny finish that most real ornaments have. If foil paper is not available, use blue paper with lick-and-stick stars for the background.

Keep the Santa simple or substitute your school mascot all dressed up for the holidays complete with a Santa hat. Add a festive greeting with lots of holly and ribbon.

<u>Merry Reading</u>

(shown on page 68)

This display is simple but makes a great wreath. Use magazine covers to form a circle. Wrap ribbon throughout the covers and tie in a big bow. Add a simple message.

MERRY READING SWAGS

(opposite)

This cheery little Santa is made from the same pattern used to make the trees in the background.

Use a sheet of newspaper to make the the tree pattern. Fold the newspaper in half and draw half the tree on the fold. Open out the pattern and trace around it on green paper for the trees.

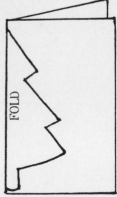

Trace the pattern on red paper for the Santa. Use white paper for the fur, beard, hair and moustache, with a small piece of pink paper for the face. Use a black marker for the details, the gloves, and the boots. Add a small construction paper book in Santa's hands and a few books gift wrapped under the tree. Add an appropriate message.

Cut while paper is still folded.

Make more to hang around the library as swags. A Santa taped on a bookend could add a little extra pizazz.

Santa taped to the end of a bookend.

MERRY

READING

MERRY CHRISTMAS...SANTA WREATH

(below)

Star Santas are very popular right now. Make a star pattern. If this is too difficult, trace around a star cookie cutter and enlarge it on the copy machine. Use this pattern so that all your Santas will be the same size.

Cut the Santas from red construction paper. Use white paper for the beard, moustache and fur. Use a black marker to color in the gloves, boots, buttons and details. Use a small piece of pink paper for the face.

Arrange the Santas in a circle. Make lots of them for a big wreath. Fill in empty spaces with smaller green stars.

Santas can be hung from the ceiling or pinned on your window blinds. Tape a straw or wire to the back of one and stick it in a plant.

WREATH

(shown on page 72)

This wreath will take some time to make. Use green construction paper and green cellophane to make the holly leaves. Cut out the holly leaf shape and cut out its center. Tape a piece of cellophane on the back to completely cover the open center space. Do the same thing with a large sheet of red paper to make the bow. Cut out sections and tape red cellophane on the back.

When you begin to assemble the wreath, pin the leaves on so that they are bent and twisted and will stand out from the wall. This will allow your wreath to be more 3-D. Add a message.

These leaves can also be pinned onto window blinds where the sun can shine through the cellophane. This gives the room a really festive feeling.

Hang leaves from the ceiling on fishing line. The hanging leaves will need to look nice from both sides. You will have to glue together two sheets of paper cut exactly the same with the cellophane in the middle.

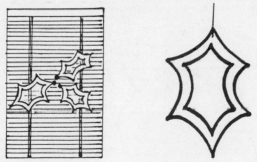

HAPPY HOLIDAYS

(shown on page 72)

Use holly leaves or evergreen trim to make a wreath. The Santa is meant to appear as though he is looking through or leaning on the wreath.

Use an 18″ × 24″ piece of red construction paper rolled and

stapled into a cylinder for the arm. (You might want to add a little newspaper stuffing to keep the arm from going flat.) Roll a shorter piece of the same color paper into a slightly larger cylinder and round-off one end to serve as the shoulder. Slide this over the top of the long cylinder.

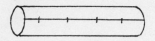 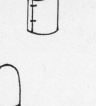

Bend the cylinder slightly for an elbow. Stuff a white glove with small pieces of newspaper. Pull it over the end of the arm cylinder and tape in place. Glue polyester fiberfil onto white paper and wrap the paper around the wrist to cover all the tape.

Use a piece of pink paper for the face. Add white eyebrows, moustache, an eye, and glasses. Use strips of white tissue paper or construction paper to create the hair and beard. Top the head off with a purchased Santa hat.

Add a book and an appropriate message, and you might add a big bow to finish off the display.

MERRY CHRISTMAS SANTA

(shown on page 74)

Use a green foil background for this silly Santa. He could even be surrounded by an evergreen or holly wreath.

Start with a circle of pink paper for the face. Add the eyes, a nose, red cheeks, a moustache and a mouth. Use strips of white tissue paper or construction paper for the hair and beard. Use a purchased Santa hat or make one from construction paper or tissue paper.

Use a pair of white gloves stuffed with small pieces of newspaper. Add a construction paper book, a holiday magazine or a Christmas card. Add an appropriate holiday message.

GIFT WRAP THE LIBRARY

(opposite)

If time is short and you really do not have room for a big display, just use some wide ribbon and "tie the library up" with big bows. Imagine the checkout desk is a gift box and wrap it with ribbon complete with a large bow and gift tag. Do the same with the ends of book shelves and doors. The bows will need to be outlandishly large to look right, but the total effect will be quite attractive. Be sure to use the same ribbon throughout. If you use lots of different kinds of ribbon in lots of different colors, the library will not have continuity.

Add a few baskets of pinecones with small, red Christmas balls sprinkled throughout, and use a bow of the same ribbon on each. These help to add color to small spaces and cost virtually nothing.

CHAPTER 6

JANUARY

NEW YEAR'S RESOLUTIONS

(below)

Use a bold color background for this first bulletin board of the new year. Use a long rectangle of white paper as the center of your display. Write your resolutions on this paper in marker or computer generate them. Try to make the print large enough to be read easily. Be sure to personalize these resolutions to fit your library. Add confetti and all types of decorations to celebrate the new year.

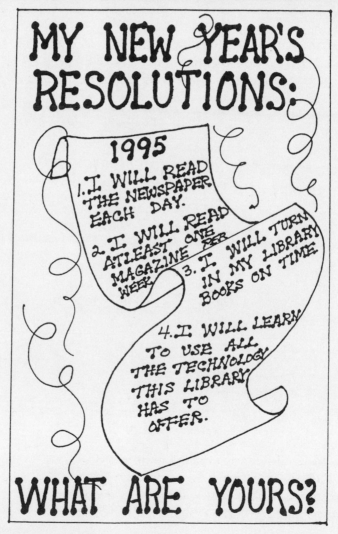

JANUARY IS NATIONAL HOBBY MONTH

(shown on page 80)

This is a fantastic way to get the whole school involved in a display. Ask your faculty and staff to tell you what their hobbies are. Print their responses and hang them from the ceiling, put them on the venetian blinds, or fill up the bulletin board. Pull books relating to the different hobbies. If you have a display case that you can lock, invite people to bring in samples of their handiwork. You will be surprised at the amount of participation from some usually passive people.

The best part of this display is the way students and faculty come together to form a common bond. You will discover that many of your patrons share the same hobby, and new friendships will develop.

Encourage everyone to develop a hobby.

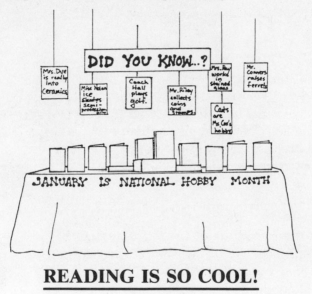

READING IS SO COOL!

(shown on page 81)

This handy little snowman fits quite nicely into any winter time display. Pull all of the books on snow skiing, sledding, winter, or basically any book that you would like to promote.

The snowman is made from a carpet tube or several oatmeal

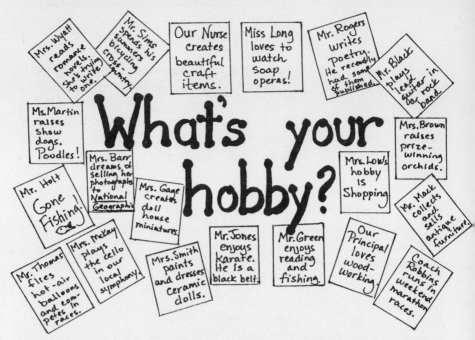

What's your hobby?

boxes taped together. Cover the tube with white paper, or paint it white if you have the time and supplies.

To create the hat, consider first the top of the hat. Trace around the end of the tube on black construction paper. Cut tabs as an extension of the circle to attach to the tube. Tape in place.

Cover the next couple of inches with a long rectangle of black construction paper.

To create the brim of the hat, once again trace around the end of the tube in the center of a piece of paper at least $9'' \times 12''$. Add two inches all around the circle. Use a compass to make this second circle.

Cut out this ring of construction paper and slide it over the top of the tube. Use a small piece of tape on the underneath side of the ring to hold it in place. A hat band of a contrasting color is a nice touch.

Cut small circles of black paper for the eyes, the mouth, and the buttons. Roll a piece of orange paper into a cone for the nose. Use a thin black marker to add a few lines to this carrot nose before you glue or tape it into place.

Use two sticks for arms. Use your scissors to punch a hole in the tube, and slide the stick in the hole and tape into place.

The boots are made from black paper and are glued in place on the tube. Fold a piece of black paper in half. Draw the boot and cut it out while the paper is still folded. This will give you two boots exactly the same size.

Use fabric or gift wrap to make a scarf for the snowman. Glue it in place. Add a sign with an appropriate message.

READING SNOWMAN

(below)

This friendly-looking snowman is great for January decorating. Begin with a dark blue background. Use a large sheet of white paper to make your snowman. You can make three circles (of snow) to build your snowman. Use construction paper, wrapping paper, fabric or even a real scarf around the neck, and be sure to add some type of hat. Use construction paper or markers for the rest of the details.

Use book covers, magazine covers, or make some construction paper books to have at the snowman's feet. Cut snowflakes and sprinkle them liberally throughout the sky and hang some from the ceiling on fishing line. Consider making the snowflake chain described in the next display.

SNOWFLAKE CHAINS

(below)

Use copy machine paper to make lots of snowflakes. Consider asking your students to cut them. You might possibly turn this into a contest. A student could add a snowflake to the chain for reading a book. He could write the title of the book read and his name on the snowflake.

Staple the edges of the flakes together to create a snowflake chain. Drape the chain around the room.

Use large sheets of white paper to create giant snowflakes to hang throughout the room. Use fishing line to hang these because it is very strong but transparent. Add a little white glitter to give these snowflakes some sparkle.

This is a "cheap" way to decorate and encourage reading.

Fold in half   Fold in half again   Keep folding in half to create a triangle shape   Fold in half again. Round off the end.

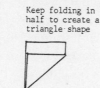

Cut out pieces to create a lacey effect.   Carefully open out to see your snowflake.

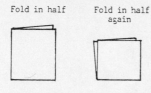

THESE NEW BOOKS ARE SO COOL!

(opposite)

Use these penguins in a table display with new books, or use them to decorate the top of a bookcase. They are easily made from a 12″×14″ piece of black construction paper.

Make a pattern for the body by cutting a piece of newspaper to be 12″×14″. Fold it in half. On the fold draw half the penguin. Be sure to extend the line to the edge of the paper. Cut this out while the paper is still folded. Using this pattern, cut a penguin out of black construction paper.

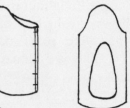

Roll the paper shape into a cylinder and staple or tape. It should now stand up on its own. Add a white triangle with the edges rounded-off for the penguin's tummy.

Add two eyes. Cut a diamond shape from orange paper for the beak and bend it in the middle. Glue the bottom half on and have the top half stick out so that the mouth will be permanently open.

Cut two orange feet and tape them to the bottom of the cylinder.

Use a sheet of black paper for the flippers. Glue one on each side and place a construction paper book in the flippers.

UNDERWATER

(shown on page 86)

Use the space at the top of the bookshelves to create an interesting underwater theme. Using fishing line, hang paper fish, nets and seaweed from the ceiling. If possible, cover any wall space in blue paper for the suggestion of water.

A fish is made from two sheets of construction paper stapled together with a small amount of newspaper inside for padding. A

fish is just a football shape with a tail and fins. Add construction paper eyes and use a black marker to draw on the scales. Glue the two larger fins on so that they can flop around.

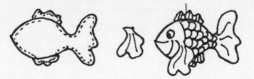

Use green crepe paper or green ribbon for seaweed. Attach one end to the ceiling and the other end to the top of the bookcase. Add a few seashells, a starfish or anything else that might be underwater for this unusual display.

It is exciting to add some pizazz to a forgotten space.

GET HOOKED

(opposite)

Reuse the fish you made for the underwater display or create this bulletin board to be used along with the underwater display. Each fish represents a type of technology available in your library.

Cut the fish out of brightly colored construction paper and display them on a blue background. Do not worry about making the fish look realistic. Silly is better. Use a dark marker to label the fish. Add some seaweed, along with a hook and a worm.

WHERE ARE YOU ON THE
INFORMATION SUPER HIGHWAY?

(shown on page 88

This is a display opportunity to call attention to your computer data bases. Use a blue background and dark letters. Use a large triangle of gray for your highway. (A piece of the ad section of the newspaper will also work.) Use a marker and a ruler to put in the dotted center line.

The road signs are just rectangles. In order for the display to look correct, be sure that the rectangles narrow as they go towards the center of the bulletin board.

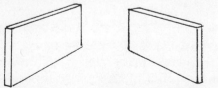

List some of your research tools on the billboards. You might need lots of billboards to feature all your library's tools.

WHY WAIT?

(opposite)

This is like a "Pow" or "Zap" in the comic books. Use a large, bright yellow explosion shape as the background for the words "Why Wait?" Use an arrow for each type of technology available in your library, and go ahead and include some other reference tools you feel all students should know how to use. The whole purpose is to encourage your students to learn how to use everything.

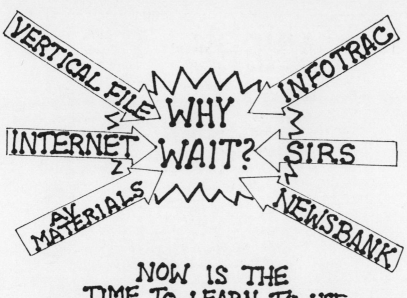

VERTICAL FILE

INFOTRAC

WHY WAIT?

INTERNET

SIRS

AV MATERIALS

NEWSBANK

NOW IS THE
TIME TO LEARN TO USE
ALL THE LIBRARY'S RESOURCES.

CHAPTER 7

FEBRUARY

CELEBRATE BLACK HISTORY MONTH

(below)

Trace around your hand and use this outline for a pattern. Since this is a celebration of Black History Month, use paper in shades of brown and black.

Arrange the hands around a world map which has been cut into a large circle. Overlap the hands. Add an appropriate message and display all types of books featuring Black Americans.

BLACK HISTORY MONTH

(above)

Use a strong light source to project someone's profile on the wall. Trace it onto some kind of paper such as newspaper or newsprint. Use this as your pattern. You might use only black construction paper or you can use shades of brown along with black. Overlap one silhouette with another. If different shades of paper are used, you do not need to have the light line between the faces. It is only used to separate one face from another when the faces are of the same color paper.

Creatively fit your letters into the remaining space. These can be uniform in size or made to fit according to the available space.

Feature books about the contributions of Black Americans in our world.

FEBRUARY IS NATIONAL
BLAH BUSTER MONTH!

(opposite)

To fight off those wintertime blues, make a display of all kinds of reminders of summer. Position it in the middle of everything.

A lounge chair makes a good display space. Add tissue paper or silk flowers for lots of color. Also add a few helium-filled balloons, a cheerful sun wearing sunglasses and a tall palm tree complete with coconuts.

The palm tree will be something to use over and over so the time spent making it is worthwhile. Call a carpet store and ask for a carpet tube. These are thrown out and are fantastic to use in library displays. Use scrap lumber to make a simple stand. Set the tube down on top of the wooden base. Nail or screw these together. Using old brown grocery bags, cut strips and clip into fringe. Wrap the strip around the tube to give the trunk of your palm tree some texture.

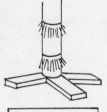

Use coat hangers that have been opened out for the branches. Fasten one end of the wire into the top of the tube.

The leaves can be made from green tissue paper, crepe paper, or green poster board. If using either type of paper, cut a long strip and fringe both sides leaving the middle section intact. Use tape to attach the paper to the wire.

The wire should remain on the underneath side. Bend the branch around to create a more realistic branch. You will probably need five or six branches.

If you use poster board, cut a large leaf shape and tape it on the wire as previously suggested.

Add some coconuts to help fill in space. These might be balloons painted brown or wadded-up brown paper lunch bags. Tape these in place on the tree trunk among your palm leaves.

Be sure to add a sign with an appropriate message because your patrons may think you have lost your mind.

AMERICAN HEART MONTH

(below)

During February display books on good eating habits and staying healthy. Use a large map of the United States for this bulletin board idea. Cut a large red heart from construction paper to cover the center of the map. Use white letters for "American Heart Month."

Contact your local branch of the American Heart Association for literature and buttons to share with your patrons.

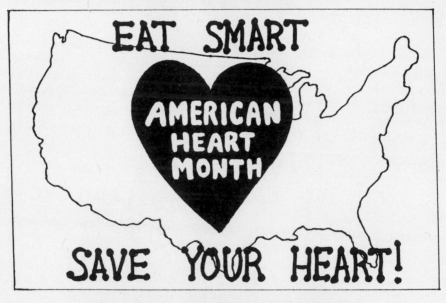

GET YOUR HEART PUMPIN'

(opposite)

Due to its simplicity, this Valentine's Day bulletin board will be one that will go together quickly.

Use a pink background or possibly some foil paper. Use red lettering and a big red heart.

If you put extensions on the heart, it will move around, and it will be "pumpin'!"

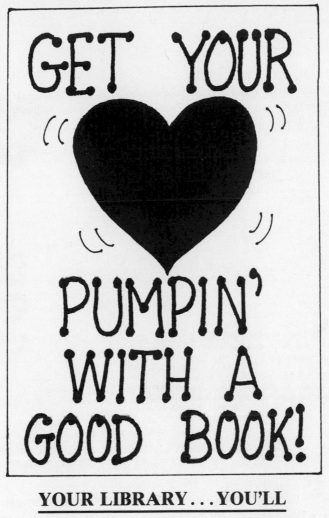

YOUR LIBRARY...YOU'LL
LOVE THE ARRANGEMENT!

(shown on page 98)

Use a pink background (paper or foil). Cut lots of red hearts for the flowers and green construction paper stems and leaves. A few red silk roses or other artificial flowers might be inserted among the construction paper hearts.

Letter different kinds of books (Romance, Mystery, etc.) on the hearts to create the arrangement.

YOUR LIBRARY...
YOU'LL LOVE THE
ARRANGEMENT!

Make a vase from any type of paper. Tie some ribbon around the vase and include a big bow. You might pretend this is an arrangement delivered by a florist and include a card in the hearts. It might say Happy Valentine's Day from the staff.

Use lots of hearts around the library. Cut some from red poster board and hang them with fishing line from the ceiling. Others can be tied together spelling out "Read" for example.

Shape a heart from a clothes hanger and tie tissue paper strips or paper ribbon around it. This could be hung from the ceiling or displayed on a door.

Be excessive—everyone likes Valentine's Day.

VALENTINE REBUS

(below)

If you do not like to cut letters, this will be just the display for you. It is adaptable to any size space. A pink background is good (paper or aluminum foil).

An eye is shaped like a football. Use a marker to add the lids, and either cut out an eyeball from construction paper or just draw one with a marker.

Lashes can be cut from paper and glued on or just drawn on with a marker.

Cut a large red heart from construction paper. If you have trouble cutting hearts, follow this plan. Fold the paper in half and draw half the heart on the fold.

Finish the display with construction paper books.

STOP...THINK...READ

(shown on page 100)

Turn your bulletin board into a giant stoplight. It is just a large black rectangle with large circles of red, yellow and green arranged vertically.

Create your own version of the road signs we see every day. Display them around your library.

LIBRARY MATH

(below)

Pretend your display area is a blackboard. Cut letters from white paper and position them on a black background. A border is optional.

Of course, you will want to make this math problem reflect the reading requirements of your English department.

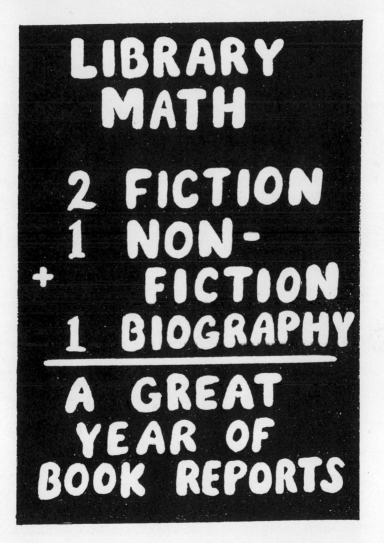

THIS LIBRARY'S COOKIN' NOW!

(below)

Need a recipe for a great year of book reports? This display can be done as a bulletin board or as a table display.

If doing the bulletin board, make a construction paper bowl, spoon, and book. Use a napkin folded around to tie all the pieces together. Use book covers from fiction and nonfiction books to include in the mixing bowl. Cut letters to create a recipe card.

Use a real mixing bowl, a spoon, and possibly some measuring cups, along with lots of fiction and nonfiction books for a table display. Use a colorful paper tablecloth on the table. Use white foam insulation board hanging on fishing line to create a large recipe card.

KEEP THE LIGHT BURNING BRIGHT

(OPPOSITE)

Use a black background and fill half the space with yellow construction paper for the light. Use white construction paper for the light bulb and aluminum foil for its base. A black marker is needed for the details, including the word "Read."

Position the light bulb on a couple of books made from construction paper or a few book covers.

CHAPTER 8

MARCH

WOMEN'S HISTORY MONTH

(below)

March is the designated month for featuring women in history. This display idea can be done in several ways. The simplest would be to use a black and white alternating scheme. Use a bright light source to project someone's silhouette on the wall. Trace it onto a sheet of paper for your pattern. Cut the silhouette from black paper and display it on white paper and vice versa.

Another possibility would be to use different colors of paper to represent all races of women. Use the silhouette pattern and create a repeat design using these colors in different combinations.

Display books featuring women and their accomplishments.

THE GALLERY

(opposite)

March is "Youth Art Month." This is a great opportunity to display artwork by your patrons.

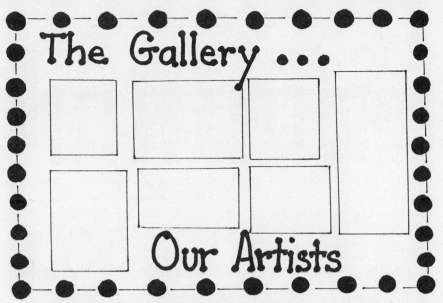

Use a dark background so the artwork will stand out. Using yellow circles to simulate light bulbs on a marquee makes an eye-catching border.

Keep changing the art pieces to feature as many different artists as possible. Be sure to keep an eye on the artwork to guard against any vandalism.

MARCH BIRTHDAYS

(shown on page 108)

This idea is adaptable to any month. Simply create a large cake and add candles for as many people as you wish to recognize.

A dark blue or black background looks good. Use whatever color (flavor) cake you like best and add the candles. Use a marker to add the name. The day of the month of each person's birthday is added to the flame of each candle. Position the candles in numerical order. These might be faculty birthdays in addition to famous people.

Add real balloons or make some balloon shapes from construction paper complete with strings. Display biographies of these people.

GOOD LUCK

(opposite)

The design for this display is simple but there are 57 letters to cut. Use a large piece of green poster board or green paper for the shamrock. Aluminum foil or foil wrapping paper looks great for the background and gives the design a little class.

Shamrocks are easy to make. Use a sheet of newspaper to make a pattern. Fold the paper in half. Draw half of the shamrock on the fold. Cut it out while the paper is still folded.

If you absolutely cannot draw a shamrock, reduce it to three heart shapes. Make these hearts meet in the middle and then add a stem.

Hang smaller shamrocks on fishing line throughout the library. Also, try stapling the edges of some together to form a shamrock chain to drape around the room.

LEPRECHAUN WINDSOCK

(opposite)

Staple a 12″×18″ sheet of green construction paper into a cylinder. Use a paper punch to punch holes on opposite sides about ¾″ from the top of this cylinder. Cover the holes with hole reinforcements. Hang the windsock with heavy-duty fishing line.

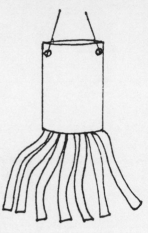

Tape or glue strips of crepe paper or paper ribbon all around the inside bottom of this tube. Be sure these strips are attached well because they will blow around when the wind catches the windsock.

Use a 9″×12″ sheet of red or brown paper for the beard. Cut as large a circle as possible making sure the edges are wavy.

Cut a smaller circle with wavy edges out of the pink paper for the face. Glue this in the center of the beard circle. Add face parts made out of construction paper, and use a brown marker to make freckles. Add a pipe.

Use black paper for a hat trimmed in green. Glue the head in place being sure to keep the top of the hat even with the top of the cylinder.

KEEP UP!

(shown on page 112)

Use colorful purchased kites throughout the room to decorate for spring. Hang them from the ceiling and attach them to the venetian blinds.

On a blue background feature kites with magazine covers attached to the tails. Drape kite string all around the display.

Encourage your students to read your magazines for personal enjoyment.

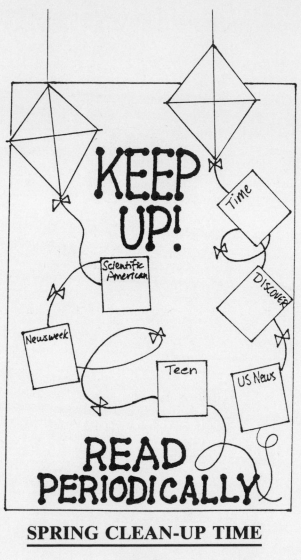

SPRING CLEAN-UP TIME

(opposite)

Turn your bulletin board into a couple of lockers. When you try to decide on the color for the locker doors, take a look in the hallway. Make them match your school's lockers.

This display is basically just three rectangles. One is a closed locker, one is a partially opened locker and one is a rectangular space for the message. Use a black marker and a yardstick to draw the lockers. Cut slits in one of the doors and slide through crumpled paper to create the illusion of a really messy locker. Using construction paper, make some simple book shapes to put in the partially opened locker.

The opened locker door may look intimidating but it is quite easy to make. Start with a rectangle the size you want your locker to be. Cut along three sides. Fold the center section back. Put in a piece of black background paper that fills up this open space. Glue in the construction paper books.

Try to make these lockers as realistic as possible. Add an appropriate message.

SPRING CLEAN-UP TIME!

PLEASE CHECK YOUR LOCKER FOR OVERDUE BOOKS.

IS IT SPRING YET?

(opposite)

In early March start pulling out any type of book that relates to spring (frogs, toads, butterflies, flowers, trout fishing, etc.).

Use a table covered with a blue sheet or blue paper tablecloth to simulate water. Use a large sheet of green construction paper cut into a circle. Cut a pie-shaped piece out of the circle to create a lily pad. Draw in the rest of the pie-shaped pieces with a black marker.

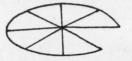

The frogs are easy to make. Use a full can of food wrapped in green construction paper for the body.

The head is one piece of green paper. Add two white circles for the eyes and two smaller black circles for the eyeballs. Draw in a mouth with a black marker. Use a dark green crayon and a yellow crayon to add some dots of color to the face.

The legs are easy to make. Fold a piece of green construction paper in half. Draw one leg on the paper and cut it out while the paper is still folded so that you will have two legs just alike. Use the dark green crayon to add spots to the legs.

Tape the legs to the bottom of the can. The full can is great to use because it has weight and will sit still on the table and not blow off. Bend the legs and pose them to hang off the table or however you want to pose your frogs.

The arms are made from green construction paper and are bent into the desired pose. Be sure to have a flap on the side of each arm to be able to attach the arm to the can body.

Use a piece of insulation foam board to create the sign which you hang on fishing line. Add construction paper letters, flowers, sunshine, and butterflies. Add whatever brings spring to your mind.

IT'S SPRING...BIG TIME!

(shown on page 116)

Everything should be exaggerated in size for this display. Keep things simple but much larger than life.

Hang a sign made of foam insulation board on fishing line.

Color is very important to the design. Make the flowers from boldly colored construction paper, tissue paper or poster board. Add a ladybug or a worm.

This is a good opportunity to display books on butterflies, insects, spring activities, and kites.

BUTTERFLIES

(opposite)

For this display, use lots of butterflies with some hanging from the ceiling and others pinned on your venetian blinds or taped directly to the window panes.

Poster board is good to use in making the hanging butterflies because of its strength and durability. It is a little harder to work with, however. Use a piece of newspaper the same size as the poster board to create a pattern. Fold the newspaper in half. Draw half the butterfly on the fold. Cut the paper while it is still folded. Open out the butterfly and trace around it on the poster board. Carefully cut out the sections in each wing. From the back, tape in a piece of cellophane of a contrasting color. The light will reflect through this cellophane and add great color to your library.

Cut two long strips of black construction paper for antennas. Glue these on the head of the butterfly.

If you would like the body of the butterfly to be black, color it in with a black marker.

Hang your creatures with fishing line. They look especially nice on windows, too.

CHAPTER 9

APRIL

APRIL IS NATIONAL HUMOR MONTH

(below)

Make a calendar with squares large enough for you to write in a daily joke or riddle. Do not put the joke or riddle on the calendar until that day so each day will hold a surprise. You might even offer a small prize for the one who guesses the answer.

To make the calendar look humorous, add a pair of large, silly red lips. The lips have to be large enough to reach the full length of the calendar. If you follow the example provided, day one and two will look like front teeth.

NATIONAL HUMOR MONTH

(opposite)

Make some large laughing mouths to proclaim humor month. Use red poster board or construction paper for the lips and tongue. Do not worry at all about realism.

Create a fun display on the top of a bookcase. Pull out all types of humorous books and encourage your students to read for pure enjoyment.

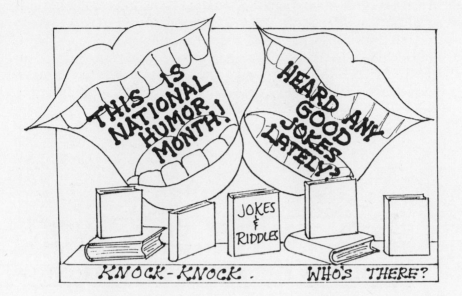

AMERICAN LIBRARY WEEK

(shown on page 122)

This can be a bulletin board or a great table display. Use a clear plastic cup or glass with a rolled-up section of the *Wall Street Journal* and a straw inside. Pin this onto the bulletin board or stand it on the table.

Use white foam insulation board for the bread of this big sandwich. The filling of the sandwich is a little of everything you have to offer in your library—a book, a CD, a computer disk, a videotape, a magazine, a cassette tape—topped with an olive (television) and a mini satellite dish. Either stack this on a plate or make some of the items from construction paper when the real items cannot be pinned on a bulletin board. Add a napkin and be sure to add a message.

READING IS THE KEY TO EVERYTHING!

(opposite)

Use a black background with a white keyhole shape added. Use a marker to add the word "Read" or cut the letters from construction paper.

Use an opaque projector to enlarge your keys to create large posterboard keys to hang around the library. Each key can feature a type of book, and it could hang in the area where that type of book is shelved.

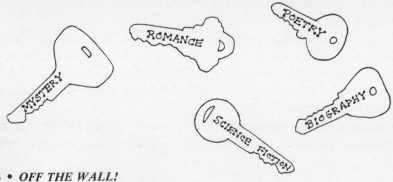

PUT YOURSELF IN JEOPARDY

(shown on page 124)

Sponsor a contest based on the television show, "Jeopardy."
Plan at least four questions each day to test the knowledge of your
students and their research abilities. Always have a special question
prepared for your faculty.

In this game the answer is given and the student must give the
question. The first one to correctly respond to all four is the winner.

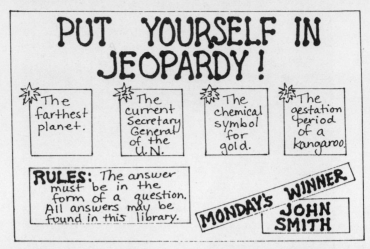

Give food coupons, ball game tickets, posters, or paperbacks as prizes.

The wonderful thing about this game is that all the questions can be answered in the library. Use all types of reference sources as you plan the questions.

Computer generate the answers and number them so they correspond with an official answer sheet that you have prepared. Display the name of the winner each day along with the previous day's correct answers. Consider using Christmas lights around the board to give the whole display that real game show look.

TIME IS RUNNING OUT!

(opposite)

To symbolize the urgency of time, use a large wristwatch. (Another idea would be to substitute an hourglass with most of the sand already in the bottom.) Use a section of a world map for the center of the watch. Draw a circle around the map with small lines added in the center to simulate minutes. Write "Earth Day" on the watch face.

Add a band. Green is a good color for this watch since it is the accepted color for living things. Add an appropriate message in bold, dark, ominous letters.

Feature a display of books on ecology-related topics. Consult your local conservation office for free literature to distribute. If your school does not already have some type of recycling project, help to organize one.

CELEBRATE EARTH DAY

(shown on page 126)

Start with a blue background and fill up the majority of space with lots of leaves, some tropical flowers, and a butterfly. The toucan bird looks harder to make than it really is. Any bird or jungle animal can be used since so many are endangered.

Use green construction paper, tissue paper or poster board for the foliage. Use a black marker to draw in details.

As you pin the leaves on the bulletin board, bend and twist them. This will create some depth and give the display a more 3-D look.

Use construction paper for the bird. It is not necessary to make the complete bird because it will be partially hidden in the foliage. Use black paper for the body.

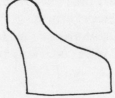

Use white paper for the front of the body and the beak. Use a black marker to draw in the lines in the beak and bright colors to color in the areas of the beak. Consult a bird book for the correct colors.

Use blue for the eye, and add the pupil with a black marker.

Use this bulletin board in conjunction with a display of books on rain forests, ecology, and recycling. It would work well with the palm tree idea previously explained.

SAVE OUR PLANET

(shown on page 128)

Recycle the palm tree described in "February Is Blah Buster Month" (see page 94). Earth Day is an important opportunity to get out all your ecology, recycling, and rain forest books for a display. Use the palm tree as a colorful addition to call attention to your books.

Be sure to add a sign with an appropriate message. The bird is not a necessity but can be made from a piece of cardboard. Paint or cover the cardboard with colorful construction paper. Substitute a snake or even a monkey for the bird if you wish.

CLIMBING THE WALLS?

(shown on page 128)

This display could fit on any size bulletin board space with any type of background. Whatever colors you decide to use, be sure that the letters really stand out.

Use old shoes from the back of your closet or visit a garage sale and pick up a few pairs. Children's shoes work great because they do not weigh much. Actually tack them onto the bulletin board.

DOES YOUR TERM PAPER HAVE YOU CLIMBING THE WALLS? ASK US FOR HELP.

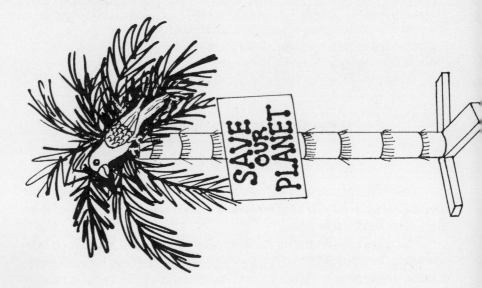

APRIL SHOWERS

(below)

There are lots of letters to cut for this display, but the total effect is very simple and the message is a good one. A simple blue background works well with whatever color letters you prefer.

These flowers were designed to represent sunflowers but any simple flowers would be great. The yellow of the sunflowers against the blue background is a great use of color and very appealing to the eye.

Add some raindrops made from construction paper, or cut up a blue trash bag for drops that are shiny and somewhat transparent.

Add as many flowers as you have special research tools to showcase. You do not have to limit your display to CD-ROM data bases. Consider adding other references like CLC, and DAB.

CELEBRATE ARBOR DAY

(shown on page 130)

Call attention to this overlooked holiday by displaying books on trees. Plan a bulletin board filled with a background of blue sky.

Reuse the tree made in "Start the Year Fresh" or make a tree from brown mailing paper or cardboard. Use a brown or black marker to simulate bark. A few simple lines can really give the bark some texture.

Use green tissue paper or construction paper for leaves. The leaves could be cut individually and pinned on or cut a whole section at one time. You might use both methods so that the display will appear to have depth. Add some extras like a kite with its tail wrapped around the tree and a bird in a nest.

Use dark letters to boldly proclaim Arbor Day. Check with the conservation department for free seedlings to hand out to your patrons.

CHAPTER 10

MAY

TAKE TIME TO APPRECIATE
THE BEAUTY AROUND YOU

(below)

Use a light color for the background. The basket is made from a large square of cardboard. Cut long strips of brown paper that you will weave together. Attach the ends to the back of the cardboard.

Make any kind of flower from construction paper. Use two or three kinds for variety. Add some green construction paper leaves. Pin the flowers and leaves on so that they are not flat. Bend and twist them to give them a 3-D look. Fill up the basket with flowers and add a few around the base.

Position the letters around the border of your display to reinforce your message. It takes time to stop and read the words, and stopping to take the time to appreciate life is what this display is all about.

WELCOME TO YOUR LIBRARY WREATH

(opposite)

Make any size wreath from construction paper or tissue paper flowers. The flowers look the most attractive and realistic when they are folded and bent to create a 3-D effect. Add a colorful bow and drape the ribbon loosely throughout the flowers.

The wreath can be made in two ways. The most obvious way would be to pin the flowers in a circle on a solid color background. Create several types of flowers—just vary the color and try to make at least three different kinds to make the design more interesting. Add leaves of different sizes to fill in empty spaces. Look at photographs of flowers in the gardening section to give you inspiration.

The other way would be to cut a circle from cardboard the size you would like your wreath to be. Cut another circle out of the center of the cardboard to form a ring. This ring will serve as the base of your wreath and will make it possible to hang the wreath on a door or a window.

Glue the flowers onto the backing. Completely cover the backing with flowers, leaves and ribbon.

WHEN I GROW UP...

(below)

Encourage your school to sponsor a career day. Invite local people from many career fields to speak to your students about their jobs (education requirements, possibilities for advancements, etc.).

Pull books on all kinds of careers and display them with the hats that these careers might require. Use some of the hats to actually hold books or let the books wear the hats.

When I grow up, I want to be a... Read more about it.

READ

(opposite)

The background for this display should be done in sky blue.

The letters of "Read" are made from polyester fiberfil because it is fluffy and "cloud-like." Fiberfil is readily available at any craft

or fabric store. Pin it into place or glue it onto a piece of paper or poster board.

Add a rainbow and a smiling sun. This is a fun way to use the word "Read" which is floating on the clouds.

EXERCISE YOUR BRAIN

(shown on page 136)

Use your school mascot reclining in a big chair as the centerpiece of this display. Include lots of books, book covers, magazine covers and newspapers. Any color background is great.

Make the chair out of flowered or striped wallpaper for contrast, or use a marker to draw lines on construction paper as pictured. If you do not want to make a chair like this, just make a big blob shape for a beanbag chair. Or, how about a hammock hanging between two trees? It makes no difference. Just be sure that the character is really comfortable and *reading*. Reading is the key.

READING QUOTE

(shown on page 136)

Use a quote about reading since that is what we as librarians need to promote. Bartlett's *Familiar Quotations* will provide many possibilities.

Use a light background and a bold color for the letters. Be sure to include the name of the person you have quoted.

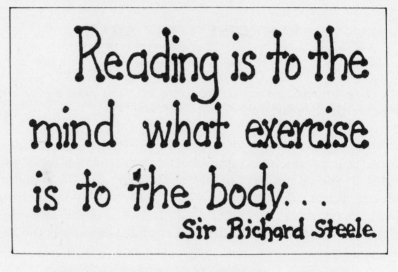

NEVER STOP GROWING...READ

(opposite)

For a long, thin display, use a blue background with a very tall flower. Any color flower will work — just make it look very cheerful. Use leaves as the hands to hold a book, magazine or newspaper.

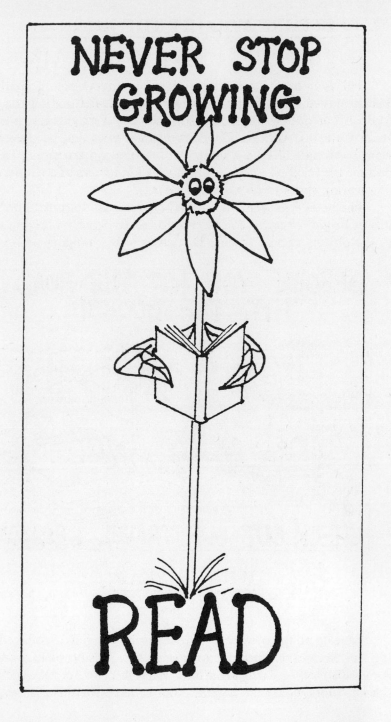

BEFORE YOU HIT THE ROAD...

(below)

This is an opportunity to display your travel books and atlases. The display might at first appear to be complicated but all you need to do is cut out photographs from some old magazines, possibly some of the old *National Geographic* magazines that people always want to donate. Make a large book from construction paper to become the focal point of the display. Add pictures of a wide variety of vacation spots to be attention-getters.

The book will seem like everything has just "popped out." Use lots of bright, cheerful colors. Try to create depth by having a few of the objects appear to be 3-D such as a fish hanging on a pole.

WHAT A YEAR!

(opposite)

Save up all the newspaper photographs you have displayed during the year and put them all up at one time. This becomes a year-in-review display. Add a message like "What A Year!" or "Wow!" Your school colors will make a great color scheme for this display.

This is a great way to end the year and will be one of your most popular displays.

HAVE A GREAT SUMMER

(shown on page 140)

Do you need an easy end-of-the-year send-off for your students? If you do, this display is it, and it is adaptable to any size or shape display area.

Use any kind of background. Light blue paper or blue plastic trash bags (opened out at the seams) look great. The neat thing about the trash bags is the shiny finish and the transparency of the blue plastic create an illusion of the sky. No border is necessary, but a simple black border would create a more finished look.

Trace a large circle on a piece of bright yellow paper. A large, round trash can works well for this. Cut enough triangles out of 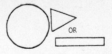 yellow paper to fit all around the circle or use rectangular strips for the rays of the sun.

Your sun needs some sunglasses. Red frames are attention-getters with the lenses made from black construction paper or black trash bags. Cut the letters for "Read" out of white paper. Use a black marker to draw in the mouth.

The letters for "Have a Great Summer" should be made of the same color paper used for the sunglasses or in black.

Use large sunglasses in other parts of the library to carry on the theme.

Make the frames from brightly colored poster board. Use a sheet of newspaper the same size as your sheet of poster board. Fold the sheet in half. Draw half of the frames on this fold. Cut it out while still folded. Use this as your pattern to trace on the poster board.

Use cellophane, dark paper, or black plastic for the lenses. Staple on the ear pieces. Add a message to the frames for an extra touch. Hang the glasses with several pieces of fishing line.

Pull out all types of books on swimming, baseball, fishing, scuba diving, travel, skin care, sun tans, and barbecues for one last display.

Encourage your patrons to read during their vacation time.

INDEX

lips 120–121
locker 112–113

March 105–117
mascot 5, 8, 9, 135–136
May 131–140
mystery 36–42

National Author Day 44–45
National Blah Buster Month 94–95
National Dog Week 27–28
National Geography Week 48
National Heart Month 96
National Hobby Month 79–80
National Humor Month 120–121
National Newspaper Week 30–31
New Year 78
newspaper 30–31, 116, 135, 138–139
November 43–55

October 29–42
ornament 63, 66–67

paint cans 19–20
paintbrush 18–19
palette 19
palm tree 94–95, 127–128
pencil 8, 9, 10–12
penguin 84–85
pumpkin 35–36, 49–50

rebus 99
reindeer 58–59
research papers 101–102
Rudolph 58–59

St. Patrick's Day 108–111
Santa 61, 66–67, 68–69, 70, 71–74
scarecrow 41–42
September 7–28

shamrock 108–109
shoes 24–25, 127–128
skeleton 40–41
snowflakes 82, 83
snowman 79–82
spider 37
spring 112–117
star 65–66, 67
star Santa 70
stoplight 99–100
summer 138–140
sun 94–95, 135, 139–140
sunglasses 94–95, 139–140
swags 14, 35, 68–69, 98

tape measure 8, 9
Thanksgiving 48–54
toucan 125–127
toy soldier 59–61
travel 48, 138
tree 63–64, 129–130
tree Santa 68–69
turkey 51–54

Uncle Sam 47

Valentine's Day 96–99
vase 97–98
Victorian Santa 61–62

welcome 12–13, 16–17, 18, 31–32, 132–
   133
windsock 110–111
Women's History Month 105
wreath 12–13, 31–32, 35–36, 51–53,
   58–59, 65–66, 67–68, 70, 71–72,
   132–133
wristwatch 124–125

Youth Art Month 106–107